Beyond Winning:

Sports and Games All Kids Want to Play

Beyond Winning:

Sports and Games All Kids Want to Play

Lawrence Rowen

Fearon Teacher Aids
Carthage, Illinois

Photographer: Andrew Forrest

ISBN 0-8224-3380-X

Printed in the United States of America
1. 9 8 7 6 5 4

To the kids, parents, staff, and director at
Peninsula School
and, always, to Sarah.

CONTENTS

**SECTION 1: WINNING THE GAME BEFORE
IT BEGINS 9**
Where to Begin? • Pregame Activities • Communication •
Choosing Sides • Overly Aggressive Players • Overly Timid
Players • Postgame Evaluation

SECTION 2: GAMES OF TAG 17
Tag Terminology • Cartoon Tag • Underdog Tag • Color
Tag • Do-si-do Tag • Color Snake Tag • Elbow Tag •
Streets and Alleys • True-False Tag • Touch-Stone

SECTION 3: BEYOND DODGEBALL 33
Crossover Rollball • Bizarre Rollball • Circle Rollball •
Super Circle Rollball • Prison Rollball • Protection Rollball •
Human Asteroids

SECTION 4: DIAMOND GAMES 45
Circle Kickball • Tunnel Kickball • Musical Kickball • Rhino
Ball • Sock 'Em

SECTION 5: GAMES PROGRESSIONS 55
Defining the Progression • Volleyball Progression •
Beachball Volleyball • Team-Catch Volleyball • Bounceball
• Sit-down Volleyball • Volleyball • Crazy Ball • Soccer
Progression • Kick-Dodge • Three-legged Soccer • Four-
Goal Soccer • Three-Four Soccer • Sock Soccer • Soccer

SECTION 6: EVEN MORE GAMES! 75
Nose Bozos • Sly Sardines • Sock Wars • Dueling Frisbees
• Bag the Flag • The Creative Olympics • Game
Committees and Experimental Games

APPENDIX: SAMPLE ACTIVITY-PERIOD FORMAT   92

INDEX OF GAMES 94

SECTION 1

Winning the Game Before It Begins

This is a book about games. More to the point, it's a book about groups playing games. It is not intended for just any group, but for the type of diverse group found in most schools, with members of all backgrounds and skill levels. And this book is not filled with just any games, but games that encourage cooperation and participation—that enhance interactive as well as physical skills. All of the games are easy to learn and fun to play. They work!

The activities in this book have been field-tested and perfected by children of all ages. Some games were originally invented by the children themselves. The activities progress from relatively simple tag games to rollball games, to diamond games, to games that lead up to popular sports, and to original game formats such as the Creative Olympics.

Where to Begin?

Although there are more than enough dynamic activities presented here to fill any activity program, a program's continued success depends on more than game selection. A few basic questions must be addressed first. What can be done, for instance, about overly aggressive players? Or overly timid players? How should new games be introduced? How can balanced teams be chosen without creating hurt feelings? Is it possible to establish a group atmosphere in which all players can excel?

This first section addresses these questions directly. It presents a variety of practical strategies that can be used to develop a safe and supportive group-play environment. These strategies constitute a necessary—and often overlooked—first step to playing games that are enjoyable for all participants— large or small, slow or fast.

By using these few well-chosen strategies in conjunction with the games and activities that follow, you can ensure success before your group even sets foot on a playing field.

Pregame Activities

A group-centered game or activity does not always begin with the first serve, pitch, or signal. Rather, it can begin earlier, often with the announcement that the time for the activity period has arrived. It is at this point, while still seated snugly in the classroom, that the participants mentally and emotionally gear up for the approaching activity. Talented athletes may begin to feel a surge of adrenaline and excited anticipation, while those less athletically inclined may begin to draw back and become less interactive. Thus, by the time the participants reach the playing area—before the game even begins—many players' attitudes have already been established.

For this reason, it is important to begin concentrating on total group involvement while you're all still in the classroom. With the announcement of the activity period, you can gather everyone together and initiate a pregame activity that involves everyone in the group.

One good idea is to gather in a circle and go around the group, allowing each member to describe in one word (or even one sound) how he or she is feeling. This sharing will encourage those who usually withdraw to express themselves at the outset of an activity period, and allow them to feel more involved.

For a less personal approach, you can have each person indicate his or her current energy level on a scale from one to ten. Or they can indicate it by raising their thumbs up high if they are "bouncing off the walls," pointing their thumbs down low if they are "almost falling asleep," or holding their thumbs at any point between the two. Whatever method of indication you choose, be sure to go around the group and give each person a chance to share. Even though some will surely ham it up when it's their turn, you'll notice that the group will begin to become more cohesive and more prepared for full group interaction.

Though the aforementioned pregame activities are both quick and effective, there are several other activities that you can use for added variety. Because the point of using a pregame activity is to stimulate total group involvement and self-expression from the outset, many different activities, such as the following examples, work well.

▼ You can play a theater game in which a player uses an object (such as a chalkboard eraser) to represent something else. Without talking, the player must act out a scene and use the object as a prop (such as passing the eraser over the hair as if it were a hairbrush or sitting on top of it and steering wildly as if it were a two-ton tractor-trailer). When another player correctly guesses what the object represents, it is passed on until everyone has had a turn.

▼ You can play a game of "Operator." Players gather in a circle on the floor and pass two different long, silly messages (one in each direction) around the circle by whispering what they hear to the player next to them. When the messages have come full circle, the last players say them aloud, often to roars of laughter (as the messages are usually nonsensical at this point). After this, the players can retrace the messages by sharing what each one thought he or she heard.

▼ You can play a rhythm game in which the group sits in a circle on the floor. One player is chosen as a "guesser" and hides his or her eyes while another is chosen as a leader. The leader initiates a certain rhythm by clapping or patting the head or patting the knees or snapping the fingers, for example. The rest of the group tries to mimic whatever the leader is doing but attempts to avoid looking directly at him or her. Once the rhythm has started, the guesser opens his or her eyes and sits in the middle of the circle. The leader changes the rhythm action (from clapping to knee patting, for instance) at regular intervals, and the guesser gets three chances to try to identify the leader. After that, a new leader and guesser are chosen, and the rhythm starts up all over again.

Communication

After a nice pregame activity, a group should be ready to progress to a successful active game or sport. Still, there are a few things to take care of before beginning the main activity.

First, set aside a short period for going over the rules of the game. Also use this period to let the players know exactly what to expect once the game begins. A few well-chosen words here will save you and the group a lot of trouble later.

For instance, if the group will be playing a silly game such as Musical Kickball or Rhino Ball (Section 4), be sure to prepare the players by letting them know it is highly likely that they will be running to the wrong bases, falling down, or just plain looking ridiculous. Let them know that it is okay for these things to occur—that you expect them to happen.

This strategy applies to virtually any concern you might have about an activity. If you are worried that players will be too rough or that there will be teasing, or if you are experimenting with a new game and are not sure if it will work, by all means tell the group! If people know what to expect—as well as what is expected of them—they can be amazingly adaptable.

Choosing Sides

The second area to cover before beginning the activity—if it is a team game—is the often ignominious task of choosing sides. Though team games can be much more fun and exciting if teams are fairly equal in ability, the process of having team captains select the teams can lead to rejection and humiliation for the players chosen last. If teams are selected randomly, however, one team can be so dominant that even a noncompetitive game can become disheartening. How should teams be chosen?

A quick technique to avoid these problems begins with each player selecting a partner of fairly equal ability (or a partner who has similar experience with or a similar attitude toward the game to be played). When everyone has found a partner, each pair of partners is split to form two equal teams. This can be done by instructing the partner with the longer socks, for instance, to go to one side of the playing area, while the partner with shorter socks goes to the other side. Because each pair of equal partners is split, two equal teams are formed instantaneously, and no undue attention is placed on individual players.

This technique for choosing sides works miraculously well! It can even become a game in itself if you use increasingly silly means to split the sets of partners, such as bushier eyebrows, birthplace closer to Philadelphia, or clothing with more colors. Feel free to experiment. No matter what criterion you use for splitting the partners, the result will always be two equal teams formed quickly.

Overly Aggressive Players

As a group begins to play an active game or sport, you should focus on maintaining the safe and supportive playing environment that has been initiated. To that end, there are certain concerns you may need to address in dealing with a typically diverse activity group.

One common concern is players who are overly aggressive or domineering. Effectively dealing with players of this sort requires some understanding of the motivations behind their actions.

Often, overly aggressive or dominant players are those who are more athletically inclined and come to the activity with more experience in traditional sports. Many players of this sort rightfully take pride in their athletic ability—even at a very young age—as it becomes an important aspect of their personal identity. Thus, their ability to dominate play—though often at the expense of others in the group—can become a validation of their own self-worth.

You can begin by offering these players the personal validation they may have been seeking through dominant play. A few well-chosen words of praise for individual players at the outset of an activity lessens the need for them to prove themselves on the playing field. Though this solution seems simple, it is often overlooked because the teacher tends to focus on those who are less athletically inclined.

Experienced players can also be appointed as "game experts." Game experts are called upon to explain rules and strategies to their teammates, as well as to make sure all players understand the game and are enjoying themselves.

Though it is important to offer dominant players validation before they seek it on the playing field through aggressive play, it is equally important to establish firm limits during the activity. Overly rough play or teasing can damage a group's cohesiveness as well as the confidence of individual players. Accordingly, it must be clear to all players that hitting and teasing are simply not allowed.

Having each player in a group agree to these ground rules as a precondition to participation serves the dual purpose of setting clear limits for aggressive players and providing reassurance for those with less confidence.

If a player forgets the ground rules or gets carried away, a one- or two-minute timeout—meted out without anger or rejection—can serve as a good reminder and even fits in well with the formats of many games and sports.

Overly Timid Players

In addition to dominant players, a diverse group is certain to include players with less confidence, who may be hesitant to participate. Often, this reluctance is due to previous difficult or painful experiences in the activity setting. Thus, these players can begin drawing back; the less one participates, the less chance there is of getting hurt.

Ironically, you should begin dealing with timid players by first dealing with the aggressive players in the group (see above). After all, no amount of encouragement or praise is going to work if players are being encouraged back into a situation in which they will be ridiculed or hurt.

Once less confident players are certain that the activity setting is indeed safe and supportive, many will rapidly proceed to take increased risks and to participate more fully. A few players may still remain hesitant or disinclined to participate, however. You can use the following strategies to help these players experience success in the activity setting.

First, individual players can set specific attainable goals to achieve during a game or sport that only they and the teacher know. Examples of such goals are rolling a ball at least five times in a game of Crossover Rollball (Section 3) or venturing off the base at least four times in a game of Cartoon Tag (Section 2).

When children experience success—no matter how small it may seem—they can begin to reverse some of the more negative patterns that may have developed for them in the activity setting.

As the program progresses, encourage timid players to expand their goals. Give them increased opportunities to express themselves during pregame activities and to introduce games of their own to the group. And, of course, offer lots of encouragement.

You will know progress has been made when it becomes necessary to use strategies designed for overly aggressive players with those whom you had been treating as overly timid. Indeed, in a supportive environment with dynamic group-centered games and activities, labels such as "overly aggressive" and "overly timid" eventually become obsolete.

Postgame Evaluation

Just as a group activity often begins well before the actual playing does, it also may not be over with the final pitch or play. As the group disbands, individual players may be walking away with concerns about other players, the game itself, or their overall experience. Left unspoken, these concerns can develop into long-standing attitudes about particular games or sports or about group play in general.

These concerns can be effectively addressed in a postgame evaluation period. A postgame evaluation enables members of the group (and the teacher) to see how the rest of the group members experienced the activity—and to compare that with their own experience. In addition, it allows players to express their opinions without either complaining or bragging.

The easiest (and quickest) way to evaluate a game is to gather everyone together in the playing area at the game's conclusion and ask them to raise their hands for one of three assessments: (1) they like the game a lot, (2) it was okay—not great but not bad, or (3) they did not like it.

If many hands are raised for categories (1) or (3), you may want to ask for some comments on what the players did or did not like about the game. The information you gain can be invaluable for planning future activities.

There are other means of conducting postgame evaluations as well. For instance, you could allow each player one word to describe his or her experience of the game. Or you could assign a small group of players the task of finding out how many people liked the game and what they did or did not like about it, and then have the group report its findings to the class. Or you could ask players to write an evaluation of a particular activity or a description of their experience in games and sports in general, and then share the results with the class.

Use a postgame evaluation after each activity—even a quick, 30-second chance to raise hands. At the very least, it will allow you to keep tabs on the progress of the group from the perspective of the players themselves. At best, it will afford the group the opportunity to define the good and to let go of the bad—leading to ever-increasing group cohesion and success in the activity setting.

SECTION

2

Games of Tag

▼ Cartoon Tag
▼ Underdog Tag
▼ Color Tag
▼ Do-si-do Tag
▼ Color Snake Tag
▼ Elbow Tag
▼ Streets and Alleys
▼ True-False Tag
▼ Touch-Stone

"Tag—you're It!" These three simple words have long precipitated raucous laughter and excitement among children everywhere. Because tag is familiar to everyone, it is an ideal game for the beginning of an activity program.

Though tag games are exciting, they can present a challenge with a diverse group. To make the games enjoyable to all, differences in speed and agility among participants must be accounted for. These differences can be handled with surprising ease if you use creative and varied approaches. Accordingly, the tag games presented in this chapter are designed to provide maximum enjoyment for children of all ages and skill levels. They progress from the gleeful frolicking of Cartoon Tag to the complex team strategy of Touch-Stone.

The atmosphere after a successful game of tag is one of satisfied exhaustion. At any stage of your activity program, a game of tag can always release energy, as well as inhibitions. Don't be afraid to use these tag games often.

Tag Terminology

The language of tag is wonderfully simple. The *It* is the one doing the chasing and tagging. The *runner* tries to avoid the It. The *base* (used in some tag games) is a designated area where runners cannot be tagged; it can be used either for strategy or merely for rest.

CARTOON TAG

Age Level: 5–8 years

Equipment: Markers for boundaries and/or base, as needed

Setup: Choose two or three Its, depending on the size of the group (one It for every six to eight runners).

Description: Cartoon Tag is a very active game that is excellent for younger groups. The game is played much like Freeze Tag. Runners who are tagged become frozen; that is, they must remain where they were tagged. Frozen runners can be freed if they are tagged by another runner.

In Cartoon Tag, a runner may avoid being tagged by quickly sitting down and yelling out the name of a cartoon. This protects the runner for five seconds (or until the It has gone away). A runner who is tagged before sitting down and yelling out the cartoon title is frozen.

Each round ends when all the runners are frozen (which rarely happens) or when the Its are too tired to continue—or when it just seems like time to change Its!

Additional Suggestions: Being chased by a maniacal It or being caught in a herd of rampaging runners can be intimidating to some children. If any runners appear tentative or scared, provide a base where they can rest and build up courage. Also, be sure the Its are gentle with their tags. If runners are bumping into one another, expand the boundaries. Either way, play this game on a forgiving surface such as mats, carpet, or grass.

If there are younger children in your group, you might ask the group to list some cartoon titles beforehand so that the younger members will have some material to call on later when the pressure is on.

Variation: Cartoons, with their silly connotations, work well as a theme for this game. But less television-minded teachers can adapt the game. "Book Title Tag" or "Planet Tag," for example, would work well. The possibilities are endless.

UNDERDOG TAG

Age Level: 5 and up

Equipment: Markers for boundaries and/or base, as needed

Setup: Choose two, three, or four Its, depending on the size of the group (approximately one It for every six runners).

Description: Underdog Tag is another variation of Freeze Tag. In this game, when a runner is tagged, he or she stands with feet wide apart, creating a one-person tunnel. Other runners may free the tagged runner by crawling through the tunnel.

Each round ends when all the runners are frozen, the Its are too tired to continue, or the Its are rotated.

Additional Suggestions: A little pregame practice to become adept at speedy leapfrogging can be helpful.

This game is fun for children of all ages, and it is one of the best activities for working off excess energy. For older or more active groups, try playing nonstop without a base—and be sure to schedule a long rest period afterward!

COLOR TAG

Age Level: 5 and up

Equipment: Field lines or cones or markers

Setup: Mark off a field (or playing area) rectangularly, 20–40 yards long and 15–30 yards wide. Choose one or two Its, depending on the size of the group (or the speed of the Its). The Its stand in the middle of the field, and the runners stand at either end of the field behind the end lines (see diagram).

Description: Color Tag is played in rounds. A round commences when the Its shout out a color. Then all runners who are wearing clothing with that color on it (visible or not) must attempt to run to the other side of the field. Runners who are tagged or run out of bounds become *frozen Its*. That is, they must remain where they were tagged (or move in bounds if they had gone out), and they are allowed to move only by pivoting on one foot. The frozen Its, as well as the original mobile Its, attempt to tag the remaining runners.

After a few rounds, a maze of frozen Its is formed. This is when the game gets really interesting. As the "octopus" of waving arms grows larger, it becomes harder for runners to cross the field. The game ends when no runners are left.

COLOR TAG

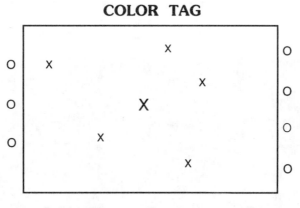

X = Original It   x = Frozen It   O = Runner

Additional Suggestions: A number of strategies can keep the game moving quickly. The boundaries can be narrowed, making it harder for the runners to get through the maze. Or a time limit can be placed on each game in order to assure that no one will have to be either It or frozen for too long.

Variations: The It can yell out other categories besides clothing colors to initiate a round. For instance, "Everyone who had cereal for breakfast!" or "Everyone born in September!" would work well. Those who fit the category must run.

DO-SI-DO TAG

Age Level: 7 and up

Equipment: Field lines or cones or markers

Setup: As in Color Tag, mark off a rectangular field (or playing area), and choose one or two Its. The Its start in the middle of the field, while the runners stand behind either end line (see Color Tag diagram).

Description: Ever been to a hoedown? This creative game, invented by children, inevitably becomes one!

The game begins like Color Tag. The original Its call out a color, and those with that color anywhere on their clothing attempt to run across the field without being tagged. When runners are tagged or go out of bounds, they become *frozen Its* and attempt to tag other runners.

When a frozen It tags another runner, however, the action really begins. Then the runner and the frozen It must perform a variation of a do-si-do, interlocking elbows as they spin once around each other. After the do-si-do is completed, the runner may continue across the field, though by this time an original (mobile) It may have caught up to him or her.

Nothing is more hysterical than watching runners trying to progress down the field while pausing to do-si-do with everyone who tags them. The game ends when all the runners have been tagged by the original Its, or when everyone is too dizzy or laughing too hard to continue.

Additional Suggestions: The narrower the boundaries, the more do-si-dos will be performed. Also, be sure to stress the silliness inherent in this activity. An overly serious player can inhibit the flow of the game. In a relaxed atmosphere, this game can be as entertaining as it is fun!

COLOR SNAKE TAG

Age Level: 7 and up

Equipment: Field lines or cones or markers

Setup: Mark off a rectangular field (or playing area), and choose two Its. The Its start in the middle of the field, while the runners stand behind either end line.

Description: This game is a variation of Color Tag. It begins with the Its calling out a color, and those players having that color on their clothing running across the field. When an It tags a runner, the It and the runner join hands and become a snake. As more runners are tagged, the snakes become longer. The game ends when all runners have joined one of the two snakes.

Additional Suggestions: As players quickly discover, this game requires a tremendous amount of cooperation among members of a snake. Be sure the group is ready for this level of cooperation before attempting to play.

A strategy that makes it easier for a snake to tag a runner is for all the members of the snake to decide beforehand which runner to chase and to call out a color accordingly. Other tips to help move the game along include making the boundaries narrower and splitting up longer snakes into more mobile smaller ones.

ELBOW TAG

Age Level: 6 and up

Equipment: None

Setup: Everybody picks a partner (you'll need an even number of players). When this is done, the partners stand side by side with their inside elbows interlocked and their outside elbows extended (see illustration). Then, all the pairs form a circle. One pair is selected to be the It and the runner.

Description: The game begins with the It chasing the runner around and through the circle, with the stationary pairs serving as obstacles. If the It tags the runner, they switch roles.

The runner can escape being tagged by locking elbows with anyone in the circle. When this happens the *partner* of the person locked on to becomes the new runner. If the It gets tired, he or she can also lock elbows with someone, and again that person's partner becomes the new It.

Additional Suggestions: To keep the game moving and to allow everyone to have a chance to run, encourage runners to lock on to someone relatively quickly. Or set a time limit of, say, ten seconds per runner.

Also, to avoid the phenomenon of only boys or only girls running, make a rule that boys must hook up with girls, and vice versa. Or enforce the rule at some times and not at others.

Despite the rounds of mandatory groans this rule often precipitates, it usually makes the game much more fun!

STREETS AND ALLEYS

Age Level: 7 and up

Equipment: None

Setup: You'll need 11 or more people. Choose one It and one runner. The rest of the players line up in rows, forming a matrix (see diagram). Each player stands an arm's length from the player on either side as well as from the player in front and behind. Select a caller (usually the teacher).

The players assume one of three positions, depending on the caller's command. If "Streets" is called, players stand with their arms out to their sides. If "Alleys" is called, players pivot a half turn, keeping their arms outstretched. If "Lampposts" is called, players stand with their arms at their sides.

AN AERIAL VIEW OF STREETS & ALLEYS

X = It   O = Runner

Streets   Alleys   Lampposts

Description: The purpose of this spirited game is for the It to chase the runner through the maze of players, never crossing between two players' outstretched arms. As "Streets," "Alleys," and "Lampposts" are called out, the group changes its formation accordingly, leaving the It and the runner in ever-changing positions in relation to each other.

If the It succeeds in tagging the runner, they switch roles. A runner may escape being tagged by switching positions with any player in the matrix. This is done simply by tapping the player on the shoulder and declaring "You're the runner!"

Additional Suggestions: The caller has a lot of control over the action in this game. The game seems to work best with a call every ten seconds or so, though unexpectedly long or short periods between calls can add to the excitement. A call of "Lampposts" can serve the dual purpose of stimulating the action (by allowing the It and the runner to run in any direction) and giving the other players a chance to rest their arms.

As in Elbow Tag, runners should be encouraged to switch places often to give everyone a chance to run, though with the exciting and often comical switches between Streets, Alleys, and Lampposts, everyone will have plenty to do!

TRUE-FALSE TAG

Age Level: 7 and up

Equipment: Field lines or cones or markers

Setup: Set up the field (or playing area) with a midline and two end lines, 25–35 yards apart. Choose two teams and a caller (usually the teacher). The teams spread out on either side of the midline, facing each other (see diagram). One team is designated the "True" team, and the other is designated the "False" team.

TRUE-FALSE TAG

	X	O	
	X	O	
	X	O	
TRUE TEAM	X	O	FALSE TEAM
	X	O	
	X	O	
	X	O	
	X	O	

Description: True-False Tag is played in rounds. A round commences with the caller yelling out a statement to both teams. If the statement is true, the True team chases the False team toward the False team's end line. All players who are tagged join the True team for the next round. If the statement is false, the False team chases the True team toward the True team's end line, and all tagged players join the False team.

The beauty of this game is that nobody loses. The game ends when everyone is on one team.

Additional Suggestions: With this activity, you can incorporate any area of the curriculum into a game format. Be prepared, though. The more confusing the questions, the more pandemonium ensues on the playing field. A pause between rounds to remind everyone which team is which and to identify which way players should run if a statement is true or false will help. Or the caller can call out a number of all true or all false statements until everyone gets used to the game.

TOUCH-STONE

Age Level: 9 and up

Equipment:
Field lines or cones or markers
A small stone, coin, or similar object

Setup: Set up the field (or playing area) with two end lines approximately 30–40 yards apart. Sidelines are optional. One team is given the stone and is on offense; the other team is on defense.

Description: This game requires a lot of strategy and cooperation. The purpose of Touch-Stone is for one player on the offensive team to carry the stone, hidden in his or her hand, across the defensive team's end line without being identified by the defensive team.

The game is played in rounds. Before each round, each team huddles for a few minutes to determine strategy. The offensive team randomly selects one player as the carrier of the stone. This player will carry it hidden in his or her fist, but *all other players will pretend to be carrying the stone as well.* The team then determines a strategy to best help the carrier of the stone make it to the other side without being tagged. The defensive team devises a strategy for tagging the members of the offensive team.

A round begins on a designated signal ("Go!" for instance). Then the action begins. Each time a player from the offensive team is tagged, he or she must stop, count to three, and then open both hands in clear view of the tagger. If the tagged player does not have the stone, *or if the defensive player does not stick around long enough to see it,* the offensive player may close his or her hands and continue running. The round ends when the player with the stone is tagged and identified, or when he or she crosses the end line. Then the stone goes to the other team.

Additional Suggestions: Creative strategy for this game is endless. The offensive team can run close together in a convoy, or spread out across the field. Players can run straight across, or have decoys go visit the lunch tables on the way over (if there is no side boundary). The defensive team can assign each player to chase a specific player on the other team, or have players patrol particular sections of the field. Or they can choose to run madly about, tagging as many people as possible.

If it becomes too difficult to successfully advance the stone across the other team's end line, try adding a second or even a third stone to the game or bringing the end lines closer together.

Be sure to stress the communication and cooperation necessary to play the game. A discussion of the entire process afterward can be very illuminating for both the teacher and the players.

SECTION

3

Beyond Dodgeball

▼ Crossover Rollball
▼ Bizarre Rollball
▼ Circle Rollball
▼ Super Circle Rollball
▼ Prison Rollball
▼ Protection Rollball
▼ Human Asteroids

Consider dodgeball. It is a perennial playground favorite and has many positive qualities. It's a highly active game that involves all the players; it encourages agility, quickness, and basic strategy decisions; and it's exciting. Yet there is one disadvantage to dodgeball that seems to be unavoidable: the sheer terror caused by balls whizzing past one's ears at ungodly speeds!

Enter the game of rollball. Rollball is a variation of dodgeball that eliminates the physical danger while maintaining the action and excitement. The central difference between the two games is in the manner in which a ball is propelled. Instead of being thrown overhand or sidearm, the ball is rolled.

This change necessitates an entirely different physical motion by players, one akin to that of bowling. Because of the motion, the ball stays low, travels at a slower speed, and is not a threat to the safety of the intended target.

Is that all there is to it? Yes! With this simple rule change, dodgeball becomes a safe vehicle for full group participation and nonstop action.

CROSSOVER ROLLBALL

Age Level: 5 and up

Equipment:
Prepainted lines or cones or markers
4–6 medium-sized playground balls

Setup: Set up the field (or playing area) as a square (10–15 yards on each side) with a line down the middle. Choose two teams, who spread out on either side of the midline. Each team begins with two or three balls.

Description: The purpose of this game is to roll the balls toward players on the other team while at the same time dodging the balls they are rolling. A player who is touched by a ball (below the knee) crosses over to the other team. The game ends when everyone is on one team.

Additional Suggestions: As for all rollball games, be sure to model the motion of rolling the ball beforehand. Also, encourage team members to take turns retrieving errant balls, so that all players get plenty of chances to roll.

To speed the game along, enact a rule that a player may hold on to a ball for only five seconds. Other options include moving the end lines in and adding more balls to the game.

BIZARRE ROLLBALL

Age Level: 7 and up

Equipment:
Prepainted lines or cones or markers
4–8 medium-sized playground balls

Setup: Set up the field (or playing area) as a square (15 yards by 15 yards) split into four sections. Choose four teams. Each occupies a square (see diagram). Each team begins with one or two balls.

BIZARRE ROLLBALL

Description: Bizarre Rollball is a variation of Crossover Rollball that allows for greater challenge and action. Players may roll balls toward opposing players in any of the squares, while dodging balls rolled at them from any other square. A player who is touched by a ball (below the knee) goes over to the team that rolled it. When only two teams are left, each can spread out into one other empty square. The game ends when everyone is on the winning team.

Additional Suggestions: Adding more balls to the game stimulates greater action and participation. A player who is touched by a second ball (or balls) before switching teams goes to the team whose ball touched him or her last.

CIRCLE ROLLBALL

Age Level: 5 and up

Equipment:
Large prepainted circle, or markers to make one
4–6 medium-sized playground balls

Setup: Everyone stands around the outside of the circle, then five to eight players (approximately a third of the group) are chosen to begin the game inside the circle.

Description: The purpose of this nonstop game is for the players outside the circle to roll the balls toward the players inside, who attempt to dodge the balls. When a ball touches someone (below the knee), he or she exchanges places with the person who rolled it. The game ends when time runs out.

Additional Suggestions: This simple, enjoyable game is appropriate for groups at all levels. It works particularly well as an introductory game for young children. To keep the game moving, use enough balls so that everyone outside the circle has a chance to roll one regularly. Foam or soft plastic balls may be used as well as playground balls.

   If it is unclear whether someone has been hit, let both the roller and the dodger be in the middle. If certain players are not getting a chance to be in the middle, rotate them in. If the dodgers are bumping into each other, expand the circle.

SUPER CIRCLE ROLLBALL

Age Level: 5 and up

Equipment:
    Large prepainted circle, or markers to make one
    4–6 medium-sized playground balls

Setup: In this game, everyone starts inside the circle. Choose two players to be outside the circle, and give them one ball to share.

Description: The game begins with the two players on the outside rolling the ball through the circle, while those on the inside attempt to dodge it. When a dodger is hit (below the knee), he or she moves outside the circle and joins the rollers. As the number of rollers increases, more balls are added to the game (about one ball for every three or four rollers). The game ends when there is either no one left inside the circle or when there are only two players left, who then become the first rollers for the next round.

PRISON ROLLBALL

Age Level: 8 and up

Equipment:
> Prepainted lines or cones or markers
> 4–8 medium-sized playground balls

Setup: Set up the field (or playing area) as a large square (25 yards by 25 yards) with a line down the middle. Choose two teams. The teams spread out on either side of the midline. Each team starts out with two to four balls (about one ball for every four players).

Description: The purpose of this game is to roll the balls toward the players on the other team, while attempting to dodge the balls they are rolling. A player who is touched by a ball goes to "prison," which is the area directly behind the other team's end line (see diagram). Players may attempt to get out of prison by retrieving the balls that roll behind the end line and rolling them toward the players on the other team from behind. If they succeed in touching someone with the ball, they are free to return to their side, while the person touched must proceed directly to prison. A round ends when one entire team is in prison. A round can go quickly, so you'll probably have time for several of them in one activity period.

PRISON ROLLBALL

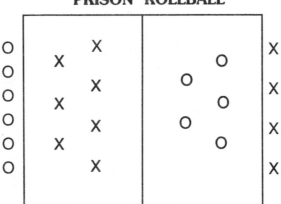

Additional Suggestions: Players should be allowed to retrieve balls only in their area; that is, they may not cross over the midline at any time or over the end line when players from the other team are in prison. To keep the game moving and to allow for maximum participation, players should not hold a ball for longer than ten seconds.

In order to help players get out of prison, enact a rule allowing them to loft balls *over* the other team in an attempt to get the balls to their teammates. Also, if some players have been in prison for a long time and the game is not ending, call a "jail break," freeing everyone in both prisons.

PROTECTION ROLLBALL

Age Level: 8 and up

Equipment:
>Prepainted line or cones or markers
>4–8 medium-sized playground balls
>8 plastic bowling pins (or similar objects)

Setup: Set up the field (or playing area) as a large square (30 yards by 30 yards) with a line down the middle. Choose two teams. The teams spread out on either side of the midline. Set up a line of four pins in the middle of each team's territory, parallel to the end lines (see diagram).

Description: This game is a variation of Prison Rollball for more advanced or more adventurous groups. As in Prison Rollball, players roll balls at members of the other team while attempting to dodge balls rolled at them. A player who is touched by a ball below the knee goes to the other team's prison. Players can free themselves from prison by rolling a ball that touches a member of the opposing team.

While all of this is going on, there is a second purpose to Protection Rollball: to try to knock over the other team's pins. This can be done by rolling balls at them, either from across the midline or from prison. A team may try to protect their pins by stopping the balls (as long as they don't use their feet). No player, however, may come within 5 feet of an individual pin. A round ends when *either* all of a team's pins are knocked over or an entire team is in prison.

PROTECTION ROLLBALL

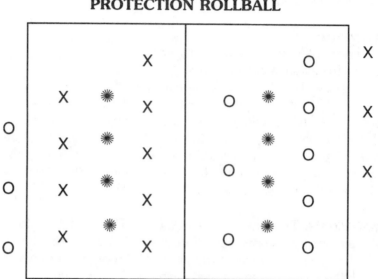

✳ = Plastic Pins

Additional Suggestions: As complex as this game may sound, it is actually quite easy to play. It does call for some interesting strategy decisions, as a team will definitely want some of its members in the other team's prison so that it can shoot at the pins from both sides.

If the rounds are moving too quickly, expand the boundaries. Or use objects that are heavier or wider than plastic pins, such as cones or pails.

HUMAN ASTEROIDS

Age Level: 8 and up

Equipment:
Large prepainted circle, or markers to make one
8 medium-sized playground balls

Setup: Mark off a small circle (6 feet in diameter) inside a larger circle. Select two players to be "spaceships." They station themselves inside the smaller circle. The rest of the players split up into pairs and become "asteroids," with each pair holding hands and stationing themselves somewhere inside the larger circle (see diagram).

Description: Are the children in your group driven to distraction by video games? Well, this game, invented by children, will allow them to play one out in real life.

The game begins with each "spaceship" being given four balls. The spaceships then roll the balls at the "asteroids," while the asteroids attempt to dodge them. If either player in an asteroid is struck by a ball, the asteroid "explodes." When this happens, the individual players in the asteroid separate, position themselves outside the larger circle, and become (believe it or not) "enemy spaceships."

The enemy spaceships collect the balls that go outside the circle and roll them back at the original spaceships. If one of the original spaceships is struck by a ball, he or she joins the enemy spaceships outside the circle. A round ends when all the asteroids have been "exploded" or when both original spaceships have been struck by enemy spaceships. Then you just put another quarter in the slot . . .

HUMAN ASTEROIDS

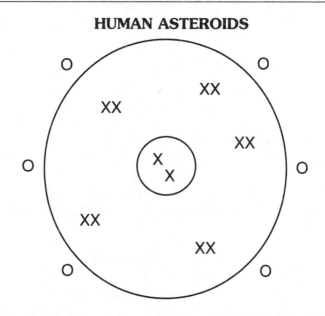

X = Spaceship   XX = Asteroid   O = Enemy Spaceship

Additional Suggestions: Before the action starts, set aside a minute for the asteroids to wander around just being asteroids, in order for everyone to get the feel of the game. Once the game has started, the original spaceships might want to refrain from rolling all of their balls too quickly. After they have rolled them all, the only way for them to get a ball back is by picking up one of the balls being rolled at them before it touches their feet. Either way, they must stay within the boundary of the inner circle at all times, unless they have been hit and are on their way to join the enemy spaceship brigade on the outside!

SECTION

4

Diamond Games

▼ Circle Kickball
▼ Tunnel Kickball
▼ Musical Kickball
▼ Rhino Ball
▼ Sock 'Em

Diamond games are a central element in the group play experience of most children. From the earliest games of kickball to later games of softball and baseball, children encounter diamond games throughout their school years.

Although diamond games can be great fun, they can also place extraordinary pressure on individual players. There are few situations comparable to being the batter in a game of softball—with all eyes, and expectations, leveled directly on you.

On top of this, inevitably some children in any group have received outside training through organized softball teams or Little League. This creates a discrepancy in experience that can make diamond games difficult to bring off successfully.

So what should you do? Should you discard diamond games from the activity program? This hardly seems fair to the group, as group members will surely be encountering diamond games in the future, and might be facing them unprepared.

Rather, the trick to introducing diamond games to a diverse group is to use activities that allow all players to be successful. In this way, you can maintain the cooperation and enthusiasm involved in a diamond game but eliminate the intimidating pressure on individual players. In a supportive environment, a diamond game can be extremely enjoyable and productive.

The following diamond games work well with both beginning and more experienced groups. They also can be used as introductory "lead-up" games for teaching softball or baseball, as will be discussed in Section 5.

CIRCLE KICKBALL

Age Level: 6 and up

Equipment:
 Premarked diamond, or four bases to make one
 Markers (or chalk) to make circle
 1 playground ball (*not* a kickball—they hurt!)

Setup: The basic setup for kickball games is the same as that for softball: a playing diamond with four bases (home plate, first, second, and third), a pitching area, outfield, and so on. For this game, outline a circle (4–5 yards in diameter) just behind second base (see diagram). Two teams are chosen, one beginning in the field and the other up to "bat."

CIRCLE KICKBALL

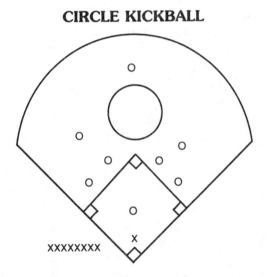

Description: Circle Kickball is designed to create action and widespread participation for the team in the field, while taking pressure off individual players on the kicking team.

 The game begins with the pitcher slowly rolling ("pitching") the ball to a kicker. When the ball is kicked, the kicker begins to run around the bases. Every base the kicker ("base runner") touches counts as one point for his or her team. Even after the base runner crosses home plate, he or she can continue to run around the bases.

Meanwhile, the fielding team attempts to retrieve the ball and stop the base runner. This is done in the following manner. After the ball has been kicked, the player closest to it retrieves it, while the rest of the team gathers inside the circle. When the entire team, including the player with the ball, is inside the circle, the team yells "Stop!" At this point the base runner is retired, his or her points are added to the team's score, and the next kicker comes to the plate.

There are no outs. An inning is over when everyone on the kicking team has had a chance to be up, at which point the teams trade positions.

Additional Suggestions: Scoring for this game should be cumulative, instead of starting the count of bases for each kicker at one and adding his or her total to the team's score. For instance, if the first kicker touches six bases, scoring for the next kicker begins at seven. Even the "final" score does not have to be final, but can be remembered and added to the next time the game is played—with the deciding game scheduled for the group's twentieth-year reunion!

Also, the fielding team can experiment with different defensive strategies. For example, the closer everyone is to the circle, the easier it is to gather there after the ball has been kicked. Not spreading out, however, allows greater opportunity for the ball to get by everyone. Either way, no player may stand inside the circle until after the ball has been kicked.

Finally, to increase the scoring—as well as everyone's feelings of success—bring the bases closer together.

TUNNEL KICKBALL

Age Level: 7 and up

Equipment:
   Playing diamond
   1 playground ball

Setup: Choose two teams, one beginning in the field and the other up to "bat."

Description: The game begins with the pitcher rolling the ball to a kicker. When the ball is kicked, the kicker runs around the bases, scoring a point for each base reached, as in Circle Kickball.

   Attempting to stop the base runner is where the action really begins. To do this, a player on the fielding team must retrieve the ball, while the rest of the players run over and stand behind him or her in a single-file line with their feet spread apart, forming a long tunnel. When everyone on the team is lined up, the player with the ball sends it back through his or her legs and into the tunnel. Each player continues passing the ball back through the tunnel until it gets to the last person, who holds the ball in the air and yells "Stop!"

At this point, the kicker is retired, and the next kicker comes up. An inning is over and the teams trade positions when everyone on one team has had a chance to kick. As in Circle Kickball, cumulative scoring is used, with each base that a player touches adding one point to his or her team's score.

Additional Suggestions: This active game requires considerable cooperation between the members of the fielding team. Thus it's a good idea to give both teams a little pregame practice forming tunnels and passing balls through them.

MUSICAL KICKBALL

Age Level: 8 and up

Equipment:
  Playing diamond
  1 playground ball

Setup: Choose two teams, one beginning in the field and the other up to "bat."

Description: This melodic game combines downright silliness with some of the rudimentary rules of traditional kickball (and softball). Musical Kickball is played much like traditional kickball with outs, base runners, runs, and so on. There are a few major, and highly entertaining, differences, however.

When a kicker has kicked the ball and is running to first base, he or she must sing a song (or at least part of one) on the way, loud enough so that at least one person on the other team can hear. And that's not all: to continue running, he or she must sing a *different* song between first and second, yet another between second and third, and so on. Of course, as in traditional kickball, a base runner may choose to stop at a base and wait for the next kicker before advancing.

A base runner who forgets to sing between any two bases is out. As in traditional kickball, outs can be scored by catching a fly ball, by tagging a runner with the ball when he or she is not on base, or by forcing a runner out at a base. An inning can be over either after three outs or after everyone has had a chance to kick.

Additional Suggestions: The great thing about this game is that the singing invariably takes the group's attention off the more competitive aspects of the game.

If you find it hard to believe that certain members of your group will actually sing out loud, remember that each player gets to choose his or her own songs. Possibilities include advertising jingles, Top-40 hits, nursery rhyme songs, movie songs—whatever appeals to each individual. Encourage creativity and self-expression; the results can be hysterical!

RHINO BALL

Age Level: 7 and up

Equipment:
    Playing diamond
    1 playground ball

Setup: Set up the bases much closer together than for other kickball or softball games. Choose two teams, one beginning in the field and the other up to "bat."

Description: This silly game can provide comic relief for groups already adept at traditional kickball. In Rhino Ball, after a kicker kicks the ball, he or she runs backward (actually turned around) to *third base,* and continues running around the bases in this manner. Outs and runs are scored as in traditional kickball. (Why the name Rhino Ball? Only the kids who invented it know!)

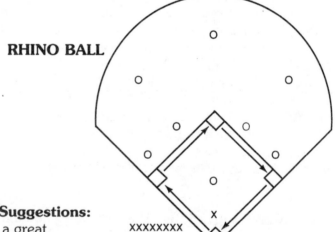

RHINO BALL

Additional Suggestions:
This game is a great equalizer because more experienced kickball players invariably make the mistake of running to first base. To avoid undue embarrassment, be sure to stress the silliness of the game while setting it up. Indeed, when the bases are loaded and runners are running backward all over the diamond, it does look pretty ridiculous! In a relaxed atmosphere, Rhino Ball can be entertaining and loads of fun!

SOCK 'EM

Age Level: 6 and up

Equipment:
Softball diamond
1 medium-sized playground ball

Setup: Choose two teams, one beginning in the field and the other up to "bat."

Description: This game was developed as a "lead-up" game for softball (see Section 5 introduction), though it is played without a bat or a softball.

In Sock 'Em, the pitcher tosses a playground ball underhand to a "batter." The "batter" hits the ball by clasping his or her hands together (as if holding a bat) and swinging at it. Outs and runs are scored as in traditional softball, with the additional rule that fielders can get base runners out by rolling the ball and hitting them (below the knee) before they reach base.

Additional Suggestions: The advantage to this game over traditional softball is that everyone can easily hit the ball, and fielding isn't quite as scary. To further alleviate pressure on individual players, an inning can consist of each player having one turn at bat, as opposed to keeping track of outs.

Variations: If you do not want to play with traditional outs and runs, or you just want some variation, Sock 'Em can be adapted to the Circle Kickball, Tunnel Kickball, or Musical Kickball formats. Or you could play a game of Circle-Tunnel-Musical-Rhino-Sock 'Em. But that, of course, is only for very advanced groups!

SECTION

5

Games Progressions

Volleyball Progression
▼ Beachball Volleyball
▼ Team-Catch Volleyball
▼ Bounceball
▼ Sit-down Volleyball
▼ Volleyball
▼ Crazy Ball
Soccer Progression
▼ Kick-Dodge
▼ Three-legged Soccer
▼ Four-Goal Soccer
▼ Three-Four Soccer
▼ Sock Soccer
▼ Soccer

Introducing more complex or difficult games presents a challenge for both teacher and learner. Improving skill and coordination, as well as simply learning rules and strategy, requires considerable practice. Traditional approaches include practice drills or skills development exercises. With a diverse group, however, practice routines can become downright boring for more experienced players and frustrating or humiliating for novices. Yet jumping right into games like softball or soccer before many children have mastered the basic skills and rules does not work either. What can be done?

Using Games Progressions is a practical solution. Simply put, a Games Progression is a gradual progression of increasingly complex games that are all related to a more difficult "target" game such as volleyball or soccer. All participants can enjoy and master each "lead-up" game before advancing to more complex or difficult activities. Though each game in a Games Progression is self-contained and enjoyable in its own right, it also provides the practice necessary for skills development. Thus, as opposed to commonly used practice routines, the more experienced players can remain interested and involved, while the less experienced players can learn gradually in a less intimidating setting.

Defining the Progression

Though the content of a Games Progression can be tailored to fit each group, a few practical steps can help you to both use the activities provided here and ultimately to design your own progressions. To maximize the effectiveness of a Games Progression, four specific steps should be included.

Step 1: Introduce the setting.

Feeling comfortable in an activity setting is a prerequisite to both enjoyment and success. To this end, virtually anything enjoyable done in the setting of the target game can serve as the first step toward mastering more complex activities in that setting.

In a Games Progression, the first step is to introduce simple games that use the setting of the more complex target game. For example, the cooperative kickball games outlined in the last section (such as Circle Kickball and Tunnel Kickball) can serve as the beginning of a Games Progression for softball. Because they use a diamond, they can introduce participants to such concepts as pitching, being "up," base running, and playing the outfield. In this way, children can learn many of the basics of softball without ever hearing the word.

Step 2: Introduce simple games that use various components of the target game.

This is the heart of a Games Progression. Playing relatively simple games and activities that include various components of the target game allows each child to master those components without being inundated by a flood of rules, strategies, and new skills to learn. These simple games also allow the teacher to easily assess the progress of the group and adjust the Progression accordingly.

An example, again using softball as the target game, would be the game of Sock 'Em (see previous section). Because players use their clasped hands to hit a large rubber ball in this game, literally everyone can master the skill of hitting the ball. This leaves players free to concentrate on strategy and team play in an activity that is less stressful than softball.

The beauty of a Games Progression is that the participants' skill and coordination levels increase because they feel safe to explore and to practice.

Step 3: Play noncompetitive variations of the target game.

Though competition can be introduced and experimented with successfully in a supportive setting, it does increase pressure and stress. This can greatly impede the growth and development of both individuals and the group. By minimizing or eliminating competition, everyone can more easily practice and master the target game.

An example, again using softball as the target game, would be to play a variation wherein each inning would be over only after everyone has had a chance to bat, instead of after each team has had three outs. Strikeouts could also be easily (and joyously) eliminated, and scoring runs could be predicated on the team solving a series of mathematical equations after the runner touches home plate. There are any number of variations that can take the focus off the score and put it on creativity and fun.

Step 4: Introduce and play the target game itself.
The success of this last step will certainly be based on the group's progress with the previous three. The group is ready to play the target game when it has successfully completed all the lead-up games. At this point, players will have already mastered the rules, strategy, and basic skills necessary to play. What a difference this makes!

The following are suggestions of Games Progressions to use in teaching volleyball and soccer. The order of the games, and indeed the games themselves, are merely suggestions. Such factors as the relative skill level, diversity, and personality of a group will ultimately determine the nature of a Games Progression. Feel free to explore—mix and match. All the games work well on their own. And, of course, have fun!

BEACHBALL VOLLEYBALL

Age Level: 8 and up

Equipment:
Volleyball court and net
1 large inflatable beachball (a spare is a good idea—they're very inexpensive)

Setup: Choose two teams. The teams spread out on either side of the net.

Description: Beachball Volleyball is played just like volleyball, though adherence to some of the finer points (such as hand positioning) is strictly optional. The light, floating action of a beachball makes this game easy for beginners to master.

As the basic rules of volleyball are not that complicated, the Games Progression should focus primarily on developing skills. To this end, Beachball Volleyball is a perfect game to begin with.

Additional Suggestions: Collective scoring (keeping track of the total number of times the ball makes it over the net in one rally) is advisable for this beginning game. It can be great fun for a group to aim for a certain target score, or set its own record and try to beat it!

VOLLEYBALL PROGRESSION
TEAM-CATCH VOLLEYBALL

Age Level: 8 and up

Equipment:
>   Volleyball court and net
>   1 volleyball or playground ball (or more for pregame
>   practice, as needed)
>   2–6 tarps, old blankets, or towels that are 3–5 feet across

Setup: Choose two teams. The teams go to opposite sides of
the net. Divide each team into subgroups of four players each
(though that can vary as needed). Give each subgroup a tarp or a
blanket, which they hold among them.

Description: The purpose of this game is for a subgroup to use
its tarp to fling the ball over the net to the other team, where
another subgroup catches it, using its own tarp.
    In order to avoid having groups crash into each other, a
number of strategies can be devised. The most obvious strategy
is to have the group that is in best position to catch the ball call
out "Ours!" so that everyone else can clear the way for them. Or
the groups on each team can rotate, with each group taking a
turn to catch and fling the ball before scrambling out of the way
of the next group. Or the court can be marked off into sections,
with one group patrolling each.
    Though this game can be scored competitively or
collectively, it seems better suited to a completely noncompetitive
approach, as it is exciting and challenging even when no score is
kept at all!

Additional Suggestions: This game requires a lot of cooperation among the members of each subgroup, and you should tell players this beforehand. A short warm-up session in which each team is given a ball to fling and catch on its own is advisable.

Variations: If the game is proving too difficult, or just for some variety, Team-Catch Volleyball can be played with a beachball or even a balloon, or it can be transformed into Team-Catch Bounceball. More adventurous groups can experiment with changes in the size of the tarp or the number of players holding it (from 2 to 20!).

BOUNCEBALL

Age Level: 8 and up

Equipment:
> Volleyball court and net
> 1 medium-sized playground ball

Setup: Choose two teams. The teams spread out on either side of the net.

Description: This game is played somewhat like normal volleyball, with one major exception: when a team has hit the ball over the net, the receiving team must let it bounce once before hitting it back. Once the ball has bounced, a team can use as many hits as it needs to get the ball back over the net.

Additional Suggestions: It is much easier to hit a ball on its way up, after it has bounced, than on its way down. This simple fact makes Bounceball ideal for developing both skill and confidence because players will experience success in keeping the ball in play. Don't hesitate to play it many times before moving on.

SIT-DOWN VOLLEYBALL

Age Level: 8 and up

Equipment:
> Beachball, volleyball, or balloon
> Markers for boundaries

Setup: Use markers or lines to make a rectangular playing area with a line down the center (there is no net). Choose two teams. The teams spread out on either side of the midline and sit down. There should be enough room between players for them to freely swing their arms.

Description: It's all in the name, though this game is far more exciting and challenging than it might seem. The two teams attempt to hit the ball back and forth to each other, with each team allowed as many hits as it needs to get the ball to the other side. Players should be allowed (in fact, encouraged) to sprawl out when attempting to get the ball. Collective or competitive scoring can be used.

Additional Suggestions: This game works well as an indoor, rainy-day activity. For some sure-fire excitement, spread the desks apart and play this game right in the classroom—with a beachball or balloon, of course.

VOLLEYBALL

Age Level: 10 and up

Equipment:
> Volleyball court and net
> 1 volleyball

Setup: Choose two teams. The teams spread out on either side of the net.

Description: If you are interested in giving your group a taste of official volleyball and you're sure they are ready for it, here are some general guidelines.

Only the team serving the ball can score points. One player continues to serve until his or her team loses a rally. When this happens, the serve goes to the other team. When a team gets the serve, the players rotate to ensure that each player will have a chance to serve. A team is allowed three hits to get the ball over the net on each volley. A game is played to 15 points.

There are many other rules for an official game of volleyball, some of which are very subtle. The aforementioned guidelines, however, should be enough to use with a typically diverse activity group.

Additional Suggestions: Before beginning to play, you might want to give each team an opportunity to warm up by forming a circle and tapping the ball to one another.

Volleyball can be a very high-pressure game, as individual mistakes are highly visible to the group. To be enjoyable to all, the atmosphere must be a supportive one. If you are disinclined to play competitively, by all means don't. Still, if the group has a knack for the game or you want to introduce it to prepare them for future play, competitive volleyball can be great fun!

Age Level: 8 and up

Equipment:
Volleyball court and net
1 volleyball

Setup: Choose two teams. The teams spread out on either side of the net.

Description: Okay, so you've tried volleyball, worked very hard at it, and are ready for a break. Crazy Ball just might be the answer.

In Crazy Ball, to be a legal shot the ball may go over, around, under, or *through* the net. It may not, however, travel *underground* beneath the net, so tunnel digging is out. A team may hit the ball on the fly, or it may let the ball bounce one to three times or five to seven times before hitting it. If a player is foolish enough to hit the ball after four bounces, everyone on the team must pull on their ears and spin around three times before proceeding. . . . Are you getting the idea?

Additional Suggestions: Completely silly games are an important part of active play and should be used regularly. Not only do they relieve tension and release energy, but they remind everyone that, after all, it's only a game!

SOCCER PROGRESSION
KICK-DODGE

Age Level: 5 and up

Equipment:
Prepainted circle, or markers to make one
2–4 medium-sized foam or soft plastic balls

Setup: Choose four to six players to begin the game inside the circle. The rest of the group spreads out evenly around the outside.

Description: The first skills to concentrate on in a Soccer Progression are controlling, aiming, and kicking a ball. This simple, fast-moving game allows participants to practice all three.

The purpose of Kick-Dodge is for players on the outside of the circle to kick the balls *on the ground* while those on the inside try to dodge them. If a ball hits a dodger below the knee, the dodger exchanges places with the person who kicked it.

Before kicking a ball, a player must bring it to a complete standstill. (This should keep the kicks low, though the balls should be soft enough not to hurt the dodgers anyway.) Players may retrieve balls kicked away from the circle, though they must dribble them back to the circle using their feet.

A few other rules can help the game along. If there is a dispute over whether a dodger has been hit by a kicker, let both of them be in the middle! In general, the more dodgers the merrier, unless they are crashing into one another. If a few players aren't getting a chance to be in the middle, establish a time limit after which they can rotate in. If many players aren't getting a chance to be in the middle, add more balls to the game.

Additional Suggestions: This game works well with younger players or beginners, who tend to kick the ball rather slowly. Still, be sure to stress that the important skills in this game are control and aim when kicking, not the speed of the kick. Take as much time as needed before the game for players to practice aiming and kicking the ball across the circle to each other, keeping the ball on the ground.

THREE-LEGGED SOCCER

Age Level: 7 and up

Equipment:
    Soccer ball
    Markers for goals
    Soft rope or fabric to tie players' ankles together (old tube
       socks or ripped-up sheets work well)

Setup: Each player chooses a partner and ties one ankle to his or her partner's ankle (three-legged style). Choose two teams using the already established pairs. Give the players ample time to choose positions and practice three-legged walking and kicking before beginning the game.

Description: This game is played just like soccer, though the three-legged element tends to make it as hilarious as it is challenging.

    Here are a couple of hints for the partners. It is much easier to move with your arm around your partner instead of at your side. It also helps to call out "step-step-step" or "one-two-one-two" until you are walking in unison.

Additional Suggestions: Stress the outright silliness of this game beforehand. In other words, players should expect to be falling all over the place! If played competitively, the game can be quite frustrating, so creative scoring of some kind might be appropriate. Also, if one set of partners is having particular difficulty, allow them to be goalkeepers for a while before gearing up for another try at running around.

If played with lightness of spirit, this wonderful game can be extremely enjoyable—and entertaining as well.

FOUR-GOAL SOCCER

Age Level: 7 and up

Equipment:
   2 soccer balls
   Markers for goals

Setup: This game is played on a normal soccer field, but instead of one goal on each end, there are two, located on the corners of the field (see diagram). Split the players into two teams, and give each team a ball to start with.

FOUR-GOAL SOCCER

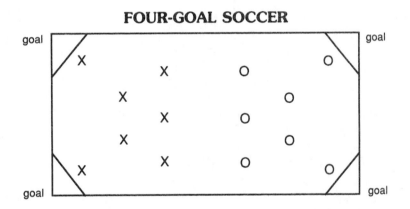

Description: Four-Goal Soccer is similar to normal soccer, with a few obvious exceptions. Because each team must defend two goals, each will have two goalkeepers. Also, a ball should be ruled out of bounds only when its placement prevents continuation of the game (under a car, for example, or in front of the principal's office windows), in which case it should be brought back to the middle of the field. After a goal is scored, the ball is immediately put back into play. Finally, a half-time break can be used to rotate player positions.

The two soccer balls encourage more action and more widespread participation. They make scoring almost impossible to keep track of, however. Don't bother.

Additional Suggestions: This game offers players an opportunity to learn and practice some of the fundamentals of soccer, while spreading out the action to relieve pressure on individual players. Important skills to stress include dribbling and control, passing the ball, and teamwork.

THREE-FOUR SOCCER

Age Level: 7 and up

Equipment:
>2 soccer balls
>Markers for goals
>Material to tie players' ankles together

Description: Combine Three-legged Soccer with Four-Goal Soccer and what do you get? Three-Four Soccer, of course.

This game is great for groups that have become proficient at three-legged movement and are ready for the increased action that two balls and four goals will surely bring.

SOCCER PROGRESSION
SOCK SOCCER

Age Level: 8 and up

Equipment:
Soccer ball
Markers for goals
1 sock (or similar-sized piece of material) for each player

Setup: Choose two teams. Each player holds a sock in one hand, with the exception of the goalkeepers. Players choose normal soccer positions (see game description for soccer on pages 73–74) and spread out for the game to begin.

Description: Sock Soccer, a game invented by a group of children, ingeniously brings total group participation to a soccer format.

The game is played like normal soccer, with the exception that when a player kicks the ball, he or she drops the sock. Here's the catch: a team cannot score a goal until all its members have dropped their socks (which means they have each had an opportunity to kick the ball). In this way, communication and cooperation become the determining factors for success!

Here are some other rules. If a goal is scored before all the socks have been dropped, it is treated as a normal out-of-bounds play. When a goal is scored after all of the socks have been dropped, the players on the scoring team must collect their socks before continuing, while the players on the other team can continue from where they left off. This should help keep the game even.

Additional Suggestions: Be sure to remind everyone to remain spread out across the field, so that you don't end up with 30 players in a massive heap around the ball, dropping socks on one another. If this becomes a problem, make a rule that each team may not have more than two players near the ball at any one time. It's truly amazing how quickly the art of passing can be learned this way.

SOCCER

Age Level: 8 and up

Equipment:
>   Soccer ball
>   Markers for goals and boundaries

Setup: Choose two teams. Players on each team assume positions including **forwards** (stay on offensive side of field), **halfbacks** (can go anywhere, but normally patrol the middle of the field), **fullbacks** (stay on defensive side of the field), and **goalkeeper** (plays in the goal and can use hands to catch or block the ball).

SOCCER KICKOFF

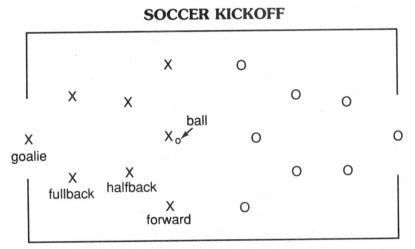

(After kickoff, forwards play on offensive side of field only.)

Description: Soccer can be a wonderfully cooperative and exciting team sport. Though, as in most sports, some rules are quite subtle, here are some general guidelines for playing soccer with a diverse group.

Kicking off:
At the beginning of the game and after a goal is scored, the
teams line up for a kickoff (see diagram). From the very center of
the field, a forward or halfback from the team kicking off begins
play by either passing the ball to one of his or her teammates or
simply kicking it downfield. After a goal is scored, the team
scored upon is given the ball to kick off.

Advancing the ball:
Players may use any part of their bodies to advance the ball
except their arms or hands. Goalkeepers (one for each team)
may use their hands as long as they are defending the goal. They
may either throw or kick the ball to advance it.

Out of bounds:
If a player kicks the ball out of bounds on either side of the field,
a player from the other team may throw it in, using both hands
and throwing from above the head. If a player kicks the ball out
of bounds across the other team's end line, the goalkeeper or a
fullback places the ball in front of the goal and is allowed a free
kick. If a player kicks the ball out of bounds across his or her
team's end line, the other team is allowed a free kick from the
corner of the field.

Additional Suggestions: Make sure everyone understands
what the different positions are and what they do. To facilitate
this, give teams ample time to meet and discuss strategy before
the game. You can designate players with league or other soccer
experience "official answer people" for their respective teams.

Finally, give lots of encouragement to the players during
the game, and ask them to encourage each other as well. A
cohesive group playing this exciting game can be beautiful
to behold.

SECTION

6

Even More Games!

▼ Nose Bozos
▼ Sly Sardines
▼ Sock Wars
▼ Dueling Frisbees
▼ Bag the Flag
▼ The Creative Olympics

The games and sports described to this point constitute more than enough material for an extended activity program. The activities are presented in a natural progression from tag games to rollball games, diamond games, and finally to more complex games and sports. Along the way, a group will discover that each activity can be successfully repeated many times, and that variations of the activities can be created and played as well.

Still, there is always room for increased variety in an activity program. Accordingly, the games and activities presented in this section can be inserted at any point in a program. They extend from rather outrageous activities such as Nose Bozos and Sly Sardines to the all-encompassing Creative Olympics. Also included are some guidelines for involving group members in activity selection and design.

NOSE BOZOS

Age Level: 7 and up

Equipment:
   3 Groucho Marx-style false noses-and-moustaches
   6 sheets of paper (or fabric) of different colors, cut into
      small pieces (the total number of pieces should equal
      the number of players; if the group has 24 members, for
      example, each sheet of paper would be cut into
      four parts)

Setup: First, choose three players as the initial "Nose Bozos,"
and give them the false noses to wear. They position themselves
in one corner of the playing area (which can be virtually
anywhere). Then, the rest of the players are each given a piece
of colored paper in such a manner that only the person receiving
it can see what color it is. Each player keeps his or her piece of
paper carefully hidden in one closed hand. Before the game
begins, players spread out across the playing area.

Description: The purpose of this rather outlandish game is for
each player to find the other players who are holding the same
color of paper—before being tagged by the Nose Bozos! To find
out the color another player is carrying, two players approach
each other and shake hands (using the hand that is not hiding
the paper). Only while shaking hands may players secretly show
each other the color of their paper. If the colors match, the
players join up with each other. If the colors do not match, the
players move on to continue their search.
   The game begins when the Nose Bozos shout "Go!" Then,
all players are free to approach each other to shake hands. In
the meantime, the Nose Bozos count to 15 and then begin to
chase after the players. Players who have already joined up
cannot be tagged. The rest of the players continue trying to
shake hands and compare colors while at the same time
attempting to avoid the rampaging Nose Bozos! A player who is
tagged stands to the side and watches the action (it won't
last long!).

A round ends when everyone either has joined up or been tagged. Then, the first three players who were tagged become the Nose Bozos for the next round.

Additional Suggestions: Encourage players to keep searching for others with the same color of paper even after they have joined up in pairs. Individual players are always free to approach an already joined pair. If not enough players are being tagged, lessen the number to which the Nose Bozos must count at the beginning of a round. If too many players are being tagged, increase the number.

As silly as this game sounds (and it looks even sillier), it is a wonderful activity to use to foster cooperation and unity. Players will find themselves happy to join up with others whom they might not normally choose to play with. And, of course, the sight of the Nose Bozos themselves is enough to lighten up any group. Take pictures!

SLY SARDINES

Age Level: 5 and up

Equipment: Places to hide

Setup: Choose two players as the initial "sardines." Give them two minutes to find a hiding place together while everyone else averts their eyes.

Description: This game is a variation of Sardines, which is a variation of Hide-and-Seek. In Sardines, after the initial sardines find a place to hide, the rest of the players split up and attempt to find them. When a player comes across the hidden sardines, he or she joins them in their hiding place. As the game progresses, more and more players discover and join the hidden sardines. Hence, the name.

Sly Sardines is a game for adventurous Sardines players. In this game, once the sardine group reaches at least three players, it can get up and attempt to slyly move to another hiding place (led by the original sardines) without being seen by the rest of the players. The sardine group continues to grow and to move stealthily to new hiding places, ducking for cover at the slightest noise, until two players are left.

A new round begins with those final two players becoming the new sardines.

Additional Suggestions: Before beginning the game, set clear boundaries within which the players can hide and search. Also, it's a good idea for the teacher to know where the original sardines are hidden, just in case a searcher gets lonely and needs a clue. After the sardine group begins to grow, however, it is more easily spotted, so this should not be a problem.

SOCK WARS

Age Level: 5 and up

Equipment:
>Prepainted lines or cones or markers for boundaries
>2 plastic or foam rods (toy bats are fine)
>Lots of socks (at least 1 per player—the ones on the
> players' feet are a good place to start)

Setup: This is typically an indoor activity played on mats or carpet, though it can be played outdoors on grass as well. Set up the playing area as a square (15 yards by 15 yards) with a line down the middle. Choose two teams. The teams spread out on either side of the midline. Choose one player on each team as the Jedi Knight, and give that player a plastic rod. The rest of the players roll the socks up into tight balls and hold them in their hands.

Description: This highly active game gets its backdrop and terminology from the *Star Wars* movie series, though in place of lasers or intergalactic photon missiles, the players' socks are used!

 The game begins with each team's Jedi Knight standing at the very back of the team's area, just in front of the end line (see diagram). The rest of the players use rolled-up socks as space projectiles by throwing them across the midline toward players on the other team. A player who is hit by a flying sock sprawls out on the floor (as dramatically as possible) and waits for the Jedi Knight to come save him or her. The Jedi Knight does this with a touch of the plastic rod, at which point the teammate comes back to life and rejoins the action.

Here's the catch: if a team's Jedi Knight is hit by a sock, he or she also must sprawl out on the floor and can no longer save teammates. A round ends when all the members of one team are on the floor.

SOCK WARS

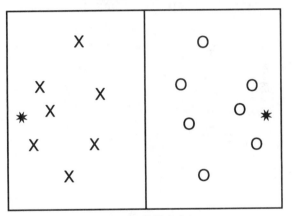

✳ = Jedi Knight

Additional Suggestions: The beauty of this game is that no matter how hard a rolled-up sock is thrown, it will bounce harmlessly off a player. In this way, players can throw and dodge and run at full speed without having to worry about being hurt. The touch of a sock can be so light, in fact, that sometimes players will not know if they have been hit. If this happens, choose a quick way to settle the question (such as a coin flip) so that it doesn't interrupt the flow of the game.

Strategy will play a part in the game as players choose how close they want to venture toward the midline (though they may never actually cross over). The closer they get, the easier it will be to throw toward members of the other team. But they will also be farther from their own Jedi Knight if they themselves are hit.

Also, a team may choose to defend its Jedi Knight by surrounding him or her with teammates (who can easily be brought back to life if they are hit by flying socks). Or a team can try for an all-out blitz of flying socks on some designated signal. If the group seems inclined to formulate strategy of this sort, leave a few minutes between each round for teams to meet and make plans.

DUELING FRISBEES

Age Level: 8 and up

Equipment:
   2 frisbees
   Markers for end lines

Setup: Set up the field with two end lines at least 30 yards apart (sidelines are optional). Select two teams. The teams spread out on either side of the field. Give each team a frisbee.

Description: This nonstop game takes the action and fundamentals of Ultimate Frisbee, which is rapidly gaining popularity on college campuses and in recreational leagues, and puts them in a format more enjoyable for less experienced groups.

   The purpose of Dueling Frisbees is for a team to toss its frisbee from one player to another down the field and across the other team's end line. A player who has the frisbee may not run or move around but rather must throw it to a teammate to advance it down the field. The other team attempts to stop the progress of the frisbee by intercepting it or knocking it down. If the frisbee touches the ground, it goes over to the other team at the point where it lands.

   The game begins with one player on each team holding a frisbee at his or her team's end of the field (see diagram). Once the game starts, the rest of the players may spread out across the field to play offense or defense or both. Players not holding a frisbee may run around freely to pursue strategic positions either by finding an open spot on the field on offense or by attempting to "cover" the other team's players on defense. At no time, however, may players hold on to other players. Also, the person with the frisbee must be given adequate space in which to throw (no defensive players within five feet or so).

   When a team advances a frisbee across the other team's end line, a goal is scored, and the frisbee goes over to the other team. As there will be nonstop, simultaneous action centering around each of the frisbees, however, it will be very difficult to keep score. Don't bother.

DUELING FRISBEES

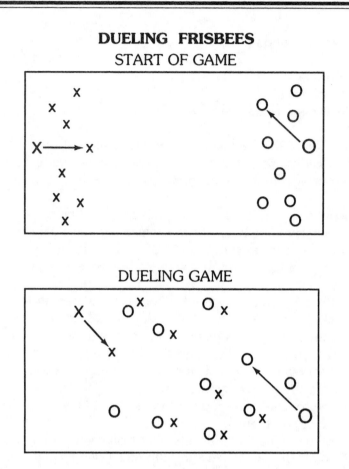

Additional Suggestions: The great thing about this game is that the two frisbees spread out the action and take attention off individual players. Players are free to run back and forth at will between the two centers of activity on the field. If very few goals are being scored, shorten the field. If too many are being scored, make it longer.

Also, before the game begins, it is a good idea to split players into small groups and let them practice throwing and catching a frisbee. Either way, be sure to let the players know that there is no great pressure to catch the frisbee every time. Players will surely be dropping frisbees all over the place, yet it only adds to the action!

BAG THE FLAG

Age Level: 7 and up

Equipment:
    Prepainted circle (5 yards across), or markers to make one
    1 tube sock or piece of sheet or fabric

Setup: Players spread around outside the circle. Place a flag (sock or sheet) in the center of the circle. Choose one player to begin the game standing guard over the flag.

Description: The purpose of this deceptively simple game is for one of the players outside the circle to venture into the circle, grab the flag, and make it back outside the circle without being tagged by the flag guard. If the flag guard tags a player inside the circle, the player must step out and count to 30 (or recite a particular passage or say the alphabet). If a player succeeds in "bagging the flag" without being tagged, a new flag guard is chosen and the next round begins. If three minutes pass and no one has bagged the flag, the flag guard is declared the winner of the round and a new guard is chosen.

Additional Suggestions: There is more potential for strategy in this game than one might expect. Individual players can make mad dashes into the circle, or they can watch and wait for the flag guard to turn away and then stealthily reach for the flag. Small groups of players can create diversions for one of their members, or they can all go in at once on a given signal.

    If players are using creative strategies and are still not able to bag the flag, make the circle smaller. If it seems too easy to bag the flag, expand the circle or add a second flag guard, or do both. If certain players are hesitant about being flag guard by themselves, add a second flag to the game and use two flag guards at a time.

Variations: If the group is a large one, you can have two games of Bag the Flag going on simultaneously. Playing this way, when players are tagged, they count to 30 and then move over to the other game and try to bag the flag there!

THE CREATIVE OLYMPICS

Age Level: 6 and up

Equipment: Will vary, depending on the type of Creative Olympic activity being played

Setup: Split players into groups of five or six. Set aside a few minutes for each group to come up with a suitably silly team name.

Description: The Creative Olympics are not so much a single game as a way of competing in which every team can win. In the Creative Olympics, teams compete in traditional and nontraditional activities and are judged not only on the basis of speed and distance, but also in the categories of creativity, style, and even silliness. Indeed, there are as many categories to be judged as there are teams competing—a not-so-subtle coincidence resulting in every team winning in a certain category.

Traditional relay-type activities played in this unique format take on a whole new look as teams attempt to figure out creative or silly ways in which to compete. Possible activities include the Wheelbarrow Race (in which a player walks forward on his or her hands while another player holds his or her feet at waist level), the Sack Race, the Three-legged Race, and the ubiquitous Egg Toss.

Nontraditional Creative Olympics activities can include the following games.

Team Ball-Carry

A team must carry a single playground ball across the field (or playing area, 15–20 yards) and back. The only provision is that every member must actively participate. (Remember all of the categories. If a team wanted to go for creativity, for example, team members could stand facing in a circle, lean over, and carry the ball with the tops of their heads while spinning their circle counterclockwise down the field! The possibilities are endless.)

Team Person-Carry

This is the same as Team Ball-Carry except that the team carries one of its own members (who can be holding a ball) across the field and back.

Seven-legged Race

Team members line up side by side. The first in line ties his or her left ankle to the right ankle of the next player in line. That player ties his or her left ankle to the next player's right ankle, and so on down the line. The first and last players will have one ankle free, and the rest of the players will have each ankle tied to one of their teammate's ankles.

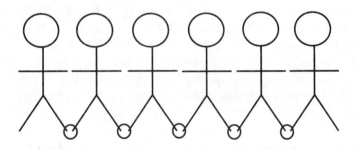

Then they have to figure out a fast, creative, silly, or stylish way to get across the field and back!

Team-Sit

After the signal to begin, each player must either sit on a teammate's lap or be sat upon, or both, with the provision that no chairs or other physical objects be used. (Doing this in a circle works well, though there is plenty of room for speed and creativity here, not to mention silliness.)

Clothes Race

Each team uses an outfit of extremely oversized clothes (pants, shirt, shoes, hat, etc.) in a relay race. Each team member must put on the clothes, run across the field (unless the team is not trying for speed), take off the clothes, and hand them to a teammate, who must repeat the process. The race ends when every team member has run.

Pyramid Race

Individual teams form either two pyramids of three players each or one pyramid of six players (or be creative if the size of the teams varies). When the teams are in pyramids, they race each other by crawling across the field, stopping to rebuild should they happen to collapse.

Under-Over

Teams stand in single-file lines with their feet spread apart. Give the player at the front of each line a playground ball. When the race begins, the player in front passes the ball backward over the head to the player behind, who then passes it backward through the legs to the next player, who passes it backward over the head, and so on. When the ball gets to the last player, he or she runs to the front of the line and begins the process all over again, until the player originally at the front of the line returns to the front with the ball.

Additional Suggestions: At the beginning of the Creative Olympics, ask for examples of creative, silly, or stylish approaches to events, so that players can get into the spirit of the activity. Then be sure to give the teams plenty of time to determine strategy and to practice before each activity.

Potential Creative Olympic activities are limitless, and a Creative Olympic program can be carried on for weeks at a time. A typical activity period might include two or three Olympic activities, plus time for practice and special exhibitions.

Finally, the teacher should judge the Creative Olympics, preferably using a secret formula of algebraic functions and subcategories that no one would even attempt to figure out. Even then, wait until the end of the entire Olympics to name winning teams in particular categories (ties are fine, too), rather than after each Olympic activity. Then have a speedy, silly, creative, and stylish Olympic award ceremony in which everybody wins!

Game Committees and Experimental Games

If you want to involve group members with activity program planning, there are several options. One is to assign a group of two to four volunteers each week to be the Game Committee. A Game Committee is responsible for selecting the activities (and having them approved by the teacher), taking care of any equipment used, and making sure that everyone has fun.

Or you can provide for experimental games that are invented by the students themselves. To include experimental games in an activity program, give groups of two to four students the task of either making up an entirely new game or a significant variation of an existing one. Experimental games can then be written up and presented in the following format:

Game Title:
Invented by:
Time Needed:
Equipment Needed:
Description of Game (rules, etc.):
Diagram or Picture of Game:

Encourage creativity, but keep in mind that the games should be attractive to a large, diverse group. If a game looks particularly difficult, have a voluntary test group play it first and then recommend whether it should be played with the whole class, modified, or abandoned completely. Once the class has produced enough experimental games, start a book!

APPENDIX:
Sample Activity-Period Format

1. Pregame Activity (in classroom—2–10 minutes)
Try to include everyone in the group. Possible activities include
a. a one-word or one-sound description of pregame feelings
b. "Operator"
c. a simple theater or word game
d. a rhythm or clapping game
e. an indication of pregame energy level

2. Game, Sport, or Activity (15–30 minutes)
Be aware of the game's atmosphere, making sure that all players are able to fully participate.

3. Postgame Evaluation (1–? minutes)
Possible means of evaluation are
a. nonverbal: Allow students to raise their hands for any one of three categories: (1) they like the game a lot, (2) it was just okay, or (3) they did not like it.
b. verbal: Allow each student one word to describe his or her experience of the activity.
c. investigative: Assign a small group of students the task of finding out how many people like the activity and what they did or did not like about it. Then have them report their findings to the class at a later time.
d. written: Assign players to write either an evaluation of a particular activity or a description of their experiences in games and sports in general. Discuss the results with the class.

INDEX OF GAMES

Bag the Flag 85
Beachball Volleyball 59
Bizarre Rollball 36
Bounceball 62
Cartoon Tag 19
Circle Kickball 47
Circle Rollball 37
Clothes Race 88
Color Snake Tag 24
Color Tag, 21
Crazy Ball, 65
Creative Olympics, The 86
Crossover Rollball 35
Do-si-do Tag 23
Dueling Frisbees 83
Elbow Tag 25
Four-Goal Soccer 69
Human Asteroids 43
Kick-Dodge 66
Musical Kickball 51
Nose Bozos 77
Prison Rollball 39
Protection Rollball 41

Pyramid Race 88
Rhino Ball 52
Seven-Legged Race 87
Sit-down Volleyball 63
Sly Sardines 79
Soccer 73
Sock 'Em 53
Sock Soccer 72
Sock Wars 80
Streets and Alleys 26
Super Circle Rollball 38
Team Ball-Carry 87
Team-Catch Volleyball 60
Team Person-Carry 87
Team-Sit 88
Three-Four Soccer 71
Three-legged Soccer 67
Touch-Stone 30
True-False Tag 28
Tunnel Kickball 49
Underdog Tag 20
Under-Over 88
Volleyball 64

About the Author

Lawrence Rowen, M.A., is an educational consultant and program administrator. He has designed and led group interactive learning and play programs in all areas of the elementary school curriculum. Lawrence has led seminars and workshops for teachers both as a school district consultant and through the University of California's Extension Program. He was a co-founder of the Quimby Summer Program for children in Sharon, Vermont. Lawrence has had a longstanding affiliation with the Peninsula School in Menlo Park, California, where he has been a teacher, administrator, and, most recently, director of its summer school. He received his Master of Arts in Education from the University of California at Santa Cruz.